EXPLORING THE STATES

West Virginia

THE MOUNTAIN STATE

by Lisa Owings

BELLWETHER MEDIA • MINNEAPOLIS, MN

Note to Librarians, Teachers, and Parents:

Blastoff! Readers are carefully developed by literacy experts and combine standards-based content with developmentally appropriate text.

Level 1 provides the most support through repetition of high-frequency words, light text, predictable sentence patterns, and strong visual support.

Level 2 offers early readers a bit more challenge through varied simple sentences, increased text load, and less repetition of high-frequency words.

Level 3 advances early-fluent readers toward fluency through increased text and concept load, less reliance on visuals, longer sentences, and more literary language.

Level 4 builds reading stamina by providing more text per page, increased use of punctuation, greater variation in sentence patterns, and increasingly challenging vocabulary.

Level 5 encourages children to move from "learning to read" to "reading to learn" by providing even more text, varied writing styles, and less familiar topics.

Whichever book is right for your reader, Blastoff! Readers are the perfect books to build confidence and encourage a love of reading that will last a lifetime!

This edition first published in 2014 by Bellwether Media, Inc.

No part of this publication may be reproduced in whole or in part without written permission of the publisher. For information regarding permission, write to Bellwether Media, Inc., Attention: Permissions Department, 5357 Penn Avenue South, Minneapolis, MN 55419.

Library of Congress Cataloging-in-Publication Data

Owings, Lisa.
West Virginia / by Lisa Owings.
    pages cm. – (Blastoff! readers. Exploring the states)
Includes bibliographical references and index.
Summary: "Developed by literacy experts for students in grades three through seven, this book introduces young readers to the geography and culture of West Virginia"–Provided by publisher.
ISBN 978-1-62617-049-0 (hardcover : alk. paper)
1. West Virginia–Juvenile literature. I. Title.
F241.3.O85 2014
974.3–dc23
                                                                                2013008955

Printed in the United States of America, North Mankato, MN.

Table of Contents

Where Is West Virginia?

West Virginia is a small state in the eastern United States. It is nestled between the northern and southern states. West Virginia shares a long border with Virginia to the southeast. In the north, the state touches Maryland and Pennsylvania. Ohio lies across the Ohio River to the northwest. Kentucky is the state's southwestern neighbor.

Charleston is West Virginia's capital city. It was built where the Elk River joins the Kanawha River in the southwestern part of the state. More people live in Charleston than in any other city in West Virginia.

Kentucky

Pennsylvania

Maryland

Ohio

Ohio River

Morgantown

Clarksburg

West Virginia

Elk River

Monongahela
National Forest

Kanawha River

★ Charleston

Huntington

N

W ✦ E

S

Virginia

History

Native American hunters followed their prey into West Virginia around 14,000 years ago. They were living in the area when Europeans arrived in the 1700s. The two groups often fought over the land. In 1861, West Virginia was part of Virginia. Virginia wanted to **secede** from the northern United States. People in the western part of Virginia disagreed. They voted to create their own state. West Virginia became the thirty-fifth state in 1863.

Native Americans and settlers

West Virginia Timeline!

1742: Coal is discovered in West Virginia.

1859: In his fight against slavery, John Brown leads an attack in Harpers Ferry. He and his men take over a building that holds U.S. military weapons.

1861: Virginia joins other Southern states during the Civil War. The western part of the state votes to side with the North.

1863: West Virginia becomes the thirty-fifth state.

1872: West Virginians approve their state constitution. This sets the basic laws and principles of their state.

1912-1921: Miners in the state fight for better conditions and higher pay. The fights are often violent.

1959: The National Radio Astronomy Observatory in Green Bank finishes building its first telescopes.

1972: A dam on Buffalo Creek collapses. The flood kills 125 people.

2006: New mining safety laws are passed after 14 miners are killed in less than one month.

John Brown

Civil War

Buffalo Creek flood

The Land

Mountains and hills shape West Virginia's rugged landscape. The entire state lies within the Appalachian Mountains. Covering the western two-thirds of the state is the Appalachian **Plateau**. This land is lowest near the Ohio River in the west. It gradually rises to the peaks of the Allegheny Mountains in the east. Mountain streams flow through dense forests toward the Ohio River.

East of the Allegheny Mountains, deep valleys cut between high mountain ridges. Rivers here run northeast to meet the Potomac. West Virginia has chilly winters and warm summers. The state gets plenty of rain, especially in the mountains. Flooding is a danger near rivers.

Potomac River

Appalachian Mountains

West Virginia's Climate

average °F

spring
Low: 41°
High: 64°

summer
Low: 60°
High: 82°

fall
Low: 43°
High: 65°

winter
Low: 24°
High: 44°

Did you know?

West Virginia is one of the most forested states in the country. Forests cover about four-fifths of its landscape.

Monongahela National Forest

Monongahela National Forest covers around 1,400 square miles (3,626 square kilometers) in the Allegheny Mountains. Red maple, black cherry, and white oak trees crowd the mountain slopes. The red spruce is also protected here. Most red spruces were chopped down for lumber by the early 1900s. The trees provide an important habitat for wildlife.

Seneca Rocks

Spruce Knob is the highest point in West Virginia. Its rocky peak lies within the forest. The trees here are bent and battered by wind. Nearby are the steep cliffs of Seneca Rocks. Several streams rush through Monongahela National Forest. They are the beginnings of the Monongahela, Potomac, and other major rivers.

Wildlife

Wildlife thrives in West Virginia. Foxes, squirrels, and white-tailed deer dart through the woodlands. In the mountains, black bears **forage** for food. Beavers and river otters play in streams. Trout, walleye, and other fish swim the rivers.

Owls and bats fill West Virginia's night skies. During the day, lucky bird-watchers might spot a ruby-throated hummingbird or cerulean warbler. These and other birds flit through forests of maple, pine, and birch trees. Tall sycamores grow along riverbanks. In summer, river valleys bloom with dogwood and crabapple trees. Nearby, rhododendrons and sweet white violets grow wild.

owl

fun fact

The Cheat Mountain salamander can only be found in the mountain forests of West Virginia. It has no lungs. Instead, it breathes through its skin!

Cheat Mountain salamander

ruby-throated
hummingbird

13

Landmarks

Harpers Ferry

Tourists find many attractions in West Virginia. In Beckley, visitors learn about the state's mining history. They can ride through the Beckley Exhibition Coal Mine and see how workers there once lived. The city's Tamarack shopping center sells products made in the state.

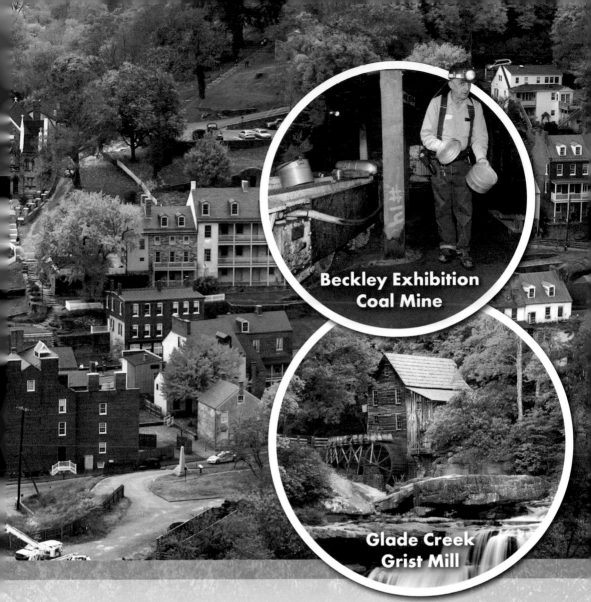

Beckley Exhibition Coal Mine

Glade Creek Grist Mill

Harpers Ferry is a historic town in northeastern West Virginia. It was an important site in the fight against **slavery** and the **Civil War**. Visitors explore the city's museums and battlefields. The Glade Creek Grist **Mill** in Babcock State Park is a favorite photo spot. In Green Bank, the National Radio Astronomy Observatory offers tours. Its telescopes see deep into space.

West Virginia State Capitol

Europeans first came to Charleston in the late 1700s. They settled where the Elk and Kanawha Rivers met. The land was rich in salt, coal, and other **natural resources**. Salt and coal mining allowed the town to thrive. Charleston was also a popular stopping point for explorers headed west.

Today, more than 50,000 people live in Charleston. The gleaming dome of its **capitol** is reflected in the Kanawha River. On warm days, people stroll or bike along the riverbanks. Charleston is also a center for arts and culture. Visitors to the Clay Center can explore art and science exhibits. They can also listen to the West Virginia Symphony Orchestra. Downtown, West Virginians enjoy art galleries, theater performances, and outdoor concerts.

Working

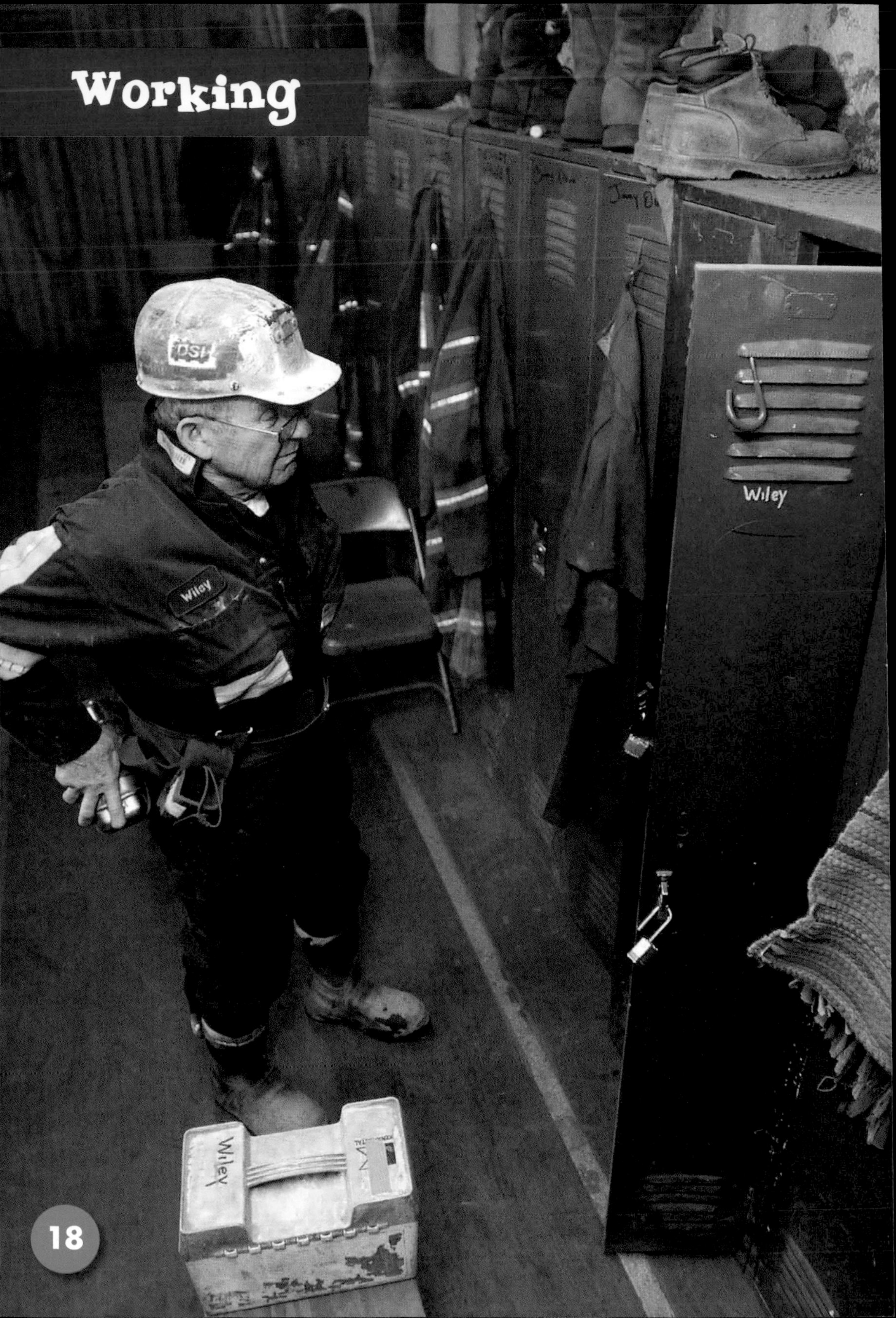

West Virginia is rich in natural resources. Workers risk their safety to dig for coal throughout the state. Oil and natural gas lie beneath western soils. West Virginians also cut down many of the state's trees to make wood products. Farmers find **fertile** land in eastern West Virginia. They grow hay, corn, and apples. Many also raise chickens, turkeys, and cows.

Factory workers produce chemicals and metals. They also make glass out of sand. Banks, technology companies, and government offices provide many **service jobs**. Other workers serve tourists as they shop, dine, and explore the state's historic sites.

Where People Work in West Virginia

manufacturing
6%

services
70%

farming and
natural resources
7%

government

Playing

The stunning mountain landscape provides year-round fun for West Virginians. In summer, they hike the Appalachian Trail or seek out cliffs for rock climbing. The state's fast-moving rivers are perfect for whitewater rafting. Those who prefer a slower pace go fishing or relax in **mineral springs**. In fall, people wander through apple orchards or take drives through colorful forests. Skiers and snowboarders can't wait for snow to cover the mountain slopes.

Many West Virginians enjoy playing and watching sports. The state has minor-league baseball and hockey teams. Basketball and football are also popular. Golfers take in gorgeous views from the state's more than 100 courses.

hiking

rock climbing

whitewater
rafting

biscuits
and gravy

Golden Delicious
apples

The first West Virginians hunted for wild **game** and fished the rivers. They gathered nuts and planted corn and beans. People in the state still work hard to put **hearty** meats and fresh produce on their tables. Biscuits and gravy, fried chicken, and country ham are popular Southern dishes. Some West Virginians enjoy deer or squirrel meat.

A favorite snack in West Virginia is the pepperoni roll. Strips of the sausage are wrapped in bread dough and then baked. In spring, West Virginians harvest wild onions called ramps. Fall brings apple season. The state is known for its Golden Delicious apples.

Pepperoni Rolls

Ingredients:

1 package of premade bread rolls, unbaked

1 package of pepperoni rounds
(sticks are okay, too)

Directions:

1. Preheat oven to 350°F.

2. Thaw rolls if frozen. Flatten each roll into a 6-inch square.

3. Layer a strip of pepperoni rounds in the middle of the dough. Lay another strip of slices next to the first.

4. Roll dough around the pepperoni. Pinch ends closed and place on baking sheet. Repeat with other rolls until baking sheet is full.

5. Bake for 30 to 35 minutes or until golden brown.

Hint: For cheesy rolls, sprinkle mozzarella cheese on top of the pepperoni before rolling. Dip in red sauce for a tasty pizza treat!

Festivals

Mountain State Forest Festival

Food festivals always draw crowds in West Virginia. Richwood hosts one of many April ramp festivals. In October, thousands enjoy a parade, contests, and fresh apple butter at Berkeley Springs' Apple Butter Festival. Italian food and music are celebrated at the Italian Heritage Festival in Clarksburg.

The Mountain State Forest Festival is one of the state's biggest events. People flock to Elkins in the fall to watch wood-chopping and fiddling contests. Other highlights include a carnival and the crowning of festival royalty. In Wheeling, the Winter Festival of Lights warms chilly crowds. West Virginians drive through a dazzling display of holiday lights.

Arts and Crafts

Early settlers in West Virginia crafted goods using the natural materials around them. West Virginians today have kept these arts and crafts alive. They make simple chairs out of maple, walnut, and hickory. Thin strips of wood are used to weave baskets. Potters turn the state's clay soils into useful tableware.

Some people create beautiful **dyes** out of walnuts, berries, and other plants. The dyes are used to color handwoven fabrics and **quilts**. Through these crafts, West Virginians are able to pass on their values of hard work and independence.

fun fact

The Cedar Lakes Crafts Center in Ripley teaches fiddling, quilting, and other skills to people of all ages. The city also hosts the Mountain State Art and Craft Fair.

Fiddlers in West Virginia are known for their skill in playing lively mountain music. The best-sounding fiddles are often carefully carved by hand.

Fast Facts About West Virginia

West Virginia's Flag

West Virginia's flag has a blue border around a white background. In the center is the state's coat of arms. A farmer and miner stand next to a rock showing the date of West Virginia's statehood. Red banners display the state's name and motto. A rhododendron wreath surrounds the coat of arms.

State Flower
great rhododendron

State Nicknames:	The Mountain State The Panhandle State
State Motto:	*Montani Semper Liberi*; "Mountaineers Are Always Free"
Year of Statehood:	1863
Capital City:	Charleston
Other Major Cities:	Huntington, Parkersburg, Morgantown
Population:	1,852,994 (2010)
Area:	24,230 square miles (62,755 square kilometers); West Virginia is the 41st largest state.
Major Industries:	mining, manufacturing, services
Natural Resources:	coal, oil, natural gas, sand, clay, timber
State Government:	100 representatives; 34 senators
Federal Government:	3 representatives; 2 senators
Electoral Votes:	5

State Animal
black bear

State Bird
northern cardinal

Glossary

capitol—the building in which state representatives and senators meet

Civil War—a war between the northern (Union) and southern (Confederate) states that lasted from 1861 to 1865

dyes—substances used to add color to something

fertile—able to support growth

forage—to look for food

game—wild animals hunted for food or sport

hearty—filling and satisfying

mill—a building that houses equipment used to grind grain into flour

mineral springs—natural pools of water that contain dissolved substances from the earth

native—originally from a specific place

natural resources—materials in the earth that are taken out and used to make products or fuel

plateau—an area of flat, raised land

quilts—warm blankets made by stitching together layers of fabric

secede—to withdraw from something

service jobs—jobs that perform tasks for people or businesses

slavery—a system in which certain people are considered property

tourists—people who travel to visit another place

To Learn More

AT THE LIBRARY

Aloian, Molly. *The Appalachians.* New York, N.Y.: Crabtree Pub. Co., 2012.

Rosenberg, Madelyn. *Canary in the Coal Mine.* New York, N.Y.: Holiday House, 2013.

Somervill, Barbara A. *West Virginia.* New York, N.Y.: Children's Press, 2009.

ON THE WEB

Learning more about West Virginia is as easy as 1, 2, 3.

1. Go to www.factsurfer.com.

2. Enter "West Virginia" into the search box.

3. Click the "Surf" button and you will see a list of related Web sites.

With factsurfer.com, finding more information is just a click away.

Index

The images in this book are reproduced through the courtesy of: Dave Sucsy Photography, front cover (bottom); DeAgostini/ SuperStock, p. 6; (Collection)/ Prints & Photographs Division/ Library of Congress, p. 7 (left & middle); Bettmann/ Corbis/ AP Images, p. 7 (right); AppalachianViews, pp. 8 (small), 8-9; Timescapes, pp. 10-11; Harrison Shull/ Aurora Open/ SuperStock, p. 11 (small), 20 (top); Bartosz Budrewicz, pp. 12-13; Rob & Ann Simpson/ Getty Images, p. 12 (bottom); Jill Lang, p. 12 (top); Svetiana Larina, pp. 14-15; Don Smetzer/ Alamy, p. 15 (top); Tim Mainiero, p. 15 (bottom); Katherine Welles, pp. 16-17; Benkrut, p. 16 (small); Rick Barbero/ AP Images, p. 18; Jeff Genter/ AP Images, p. 19 (small); Robert Pernell, pp. 20-21; Corey Rich/ Aurora Open/ SuperStock, p. 20 (bottom); RoJo Images, p. 22; Olga Lyubkina, p. 22 (small); Charles Brutlag, p. 23; Scott J. Ferrell/ Congressional Quarterly/ Newscom, pp. 24-25; Philip Wolmuth/ Alamy, pp. 26-27; H. Mark Weidman Photography/ Alamy, p. 26 (top); Bob Pardue/ Alamy, p. 26 (bottom); Pakmor, p. 28 (top); JayL, p. 28 (bottom); Denis Tabler, p. 29 (left); Sari Oneal, p. 29 (right).